Montessori
Pink Series
Reading Workbook

an open-and-go solution for teaching beginning reading the Montessori way

- ✓ read 3 letter phonetic words
- ✓ read short phrases
- ✓ read full sentences
- ✓ read full books
- ✓ practice handwriting on lined and unlined paper
- ✓ strengthen hand muscles through drawing, tracing and shading
- ✓ encourage creativity and freedom of expression through writing prompts and real-life list making
- ✓ options for non-writers

by Katie Key
montessoriforhomeschoolers.com

Copyright © 2020. Katie Key.
All rights reserved.
No part of this publication may be reproduced, stored in a retrieval system or transmitted in any form or by any means – electronic, mechanical, photocopying, and recording or otherwise – without prior written permission from the author. To perform any of the above is an infringement of copyright law.

Handwriting Font Credit: KG Primary Italics Regular

ISBN: 978-1-7353980-1-3
Library of Congress Control Number: 1-10025897821

Montessori Pink Series Reading Workbook

montessoriforhomeschoolers.com

Table of Contents

Introduction 1
   Is My Student Ready for this Workbook? 1
   Pre-Test and Remediation 1
   Two Master Rules for Teaching Reading 2
   Handwriting and Sound Recognition Chart 3
   Transitioning from Letter Sounds to Building Words 4
   Handwriting 5
   Getting Started 6
   A Special Note on Reading Aloud 6

Unit 1 7
   Lesson 1.1 Picture to Word Matching 9
   Lesson 1.2 Word to Picture Matching 10
   Lesson 1.3 Word Writing 11
   Lesson 1.4 Word Writing 12
   Lesson 1.5 Secret Words 13
   Lesson 1.6 Action Game 14
   Lesson 1.7 Pink Booklet 1 15
   Lesson 1.8 Draw and Write 17
   Lesson 1.9 Make a List 18

Unit 2 19
   Lesson 2.1 Picture to Word Matching 21
   Lesson 2.2 Word to Picture Matching 22
   Lesson 2.3 Word Writing 23
   Lesson 2.4 Word Writing 24
   Lesson 2.5 Secret Words 25
   Lesson 2.6 Action Game 26
   Lesson 2.7 Pink Booklet 2 27
   Lesson 2.8 Draw and Write 29
   Lesson 2.9 Make a List 30

Unit 3 31
   Lesson 3.1 Picture to Word Matching 33
   Lesson 3.2 Word to Picture Matching 34
   Lesson 3.3 Word Writing 35
   Lesson 3.4 Word Writing 36
   Lesson 3.5 Secret Words 37
   Lesson 3.6 Action Game 38
   Lesson 3.7 Pink Booklet 3 39
   Lesson 3.8 Draw and Write 41
   Lesson 3.9 Make a List 42

Unit 4 43
   Lesson 4.1 Picture to Word Matching 45
   Lesson 4.2 Word to Picture Matching 46
   Lesson 4.3 Word Writing 47
   Lesson 4.4 Word Writing 48
   Lesson 4.5 Secret Words 49
   Lesson 4.6 Action Game 50
   Lesson 4.7 Pink Booklet 4 51
   Lesson 4.8 Draw and Write 53
   Lesson 4.9 Make a List 54

Unit 5 55
   Lesson 5.1 Picture to Word Matching 57
   Lesson 5.2 Word to Picture Matching 58
   Lesson 5.3 Word Writing 59
   Lesson 5.4 Word Writing 60
   Lesson 5.5 Secret Words 61
   Lesson 5.6 Action Game 62
   Lesson 5.7 Pink Booklet 5 63
   Lesson 5.8 Draw and Write 64
   Lesson 5.9 Make a List 65

Unit 6 67
   Lesson 6.1 Reading Lists 1 & 2 67
   Lesson 6.2 Reading Lists 3 & 4 68
   Lesson 6.3 Reading Lists 5 & 6 69
   Lesson 6.4 Reading Lists 7 & 8 70
   Lesson 6.5 Reading List 9 71
   Lesson 6.6 Picture to Phrase Match 73
   Lesson 6.7 Phrase to Picture Match 74
   Lesson 6.8 I Can Read: Book 1, "Tom" 75
   Lesson 6.9 Picture to Phrase Match 79
   Lesson 6.10 Phrase to Picture Match 80
   Lesson 6.11 I Can Read: Book 2, "Peg" 81
   Lesson 6.12 Picture to Phrase Match 85
   Lesson 6.13 Phrase to Picture Match 86
   Lesson 6.14 I Can Read: Book 3, "Jan" 87

Completion Certificate 91
Handwriting Chart 93
Other Publications 95

Introduction

Dear Educator,

Thank you for purchasing this Montessori-inspired open-and-go reading workbook! Within the pages of this text, you will find everything you need to help your student advance from recognizing single letter sounds and building words to reading simple phonetic sentences.

These activities were created with the homeschooler in mind, but they can easily be adapted to a school setting. You can use these activities with one child or multiple children.

My prayer is that as you are working with your student, you will build a stronger relationship in each lesson. With that being said, feel free to slow down or speed up to match your student's pace. Start with a five minute lesson and work your way up to fifteen minutes slowly. On the flip side, if your student is immersed in a lesson, don't interrupt her! Let her work independently for as long as she desires!

You can find more of my Montessori-inspired resources at montessoriforhomeschoolers.com, including a digital version of this book, the pre-requisite to this book called, "Montessori Reading Games - Level 1," open-and-go Montessori math workbooks, and a full Montessori Christian homeschool preschool curriculum.

May God Bless You and Yours,

Katie Key

Is My Student Ready for this Workbook?

In this Workbook, we jump right into reading CVC words (Consonant - Vowel - Consonant.) Your child should know all 25 phonetic sounds found in the American alphabet. We don't use "q" yet since it is a double-letter sound (qu). Only one phoneme is used per letter. **Your child is not expected to know the names of the letters, just the sounds.** In fact, writing and reading will come much more quickly and easily if your child first learns the *sounds* of each letter and learns the names later on. Here is a list of the sounds used in the workbook:

a - apple	f - fox	k - kit	p - pig	v - van
b - bat	g - goat	l - lamp	r - rug	w - water
c - cat	h - hat	m - mud	s - sit	x - fox
d - dog	i - igloo	n - nut	t - tug	y - yam
e - elephant	j - jam	o - octopus	u - umbrella	z - zebra

Pre-Test and Remediation

You can use the following page to "test" your student's knowledge of each sound by sight. Feel free to invite your student to "read" each sound or make it a game by using BINGO chips and calling out each sound out of order.

If your child does not know all of the sounds, I recommend starting with the **Montessori Reading Games - Level 1** that can be found in my online shop (montessoriforhomeschoolers.com). It is a series of games that progressively introduces all of the sounds of the letters of the alphabet. Some reading is suggested, but it is mainly a beginning phonics program.

This workbook is the "next step" after the **Montessori Reading Games - Level 1.**

If you're just looking for a quick review, then use a set of sandpaper letters to introduce each sound. (You can homemake them using neat handwriting, a pack of 3x5 index cards, and a tube of glitter glue!) **Use the three-period lesson for mastery.**

Montessori 3-Period Lesson

Period 1: Introduce 2-3 letters in one sitting. ("This says, /b/."
Then have your child trace the letter three times with her pointer and middle fingers as she says the sound /b/.)
Period 2: "Show me." (Say, "Show me /b./")
Period 3: "Tell me." (Ask, "What is this?")

Spend some time each day introducing new letters and reviewing previous letters until all 25 sounds have been mastered. If you need extra practice, you will find plenty in the **Montessori Reading Games - Level 1.**

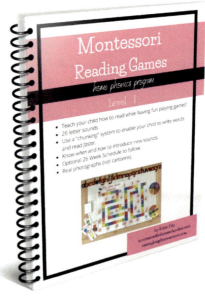

2

Handwriting and Sound Recognition Chart

a	e	i	o	u
b	c	d	f	g
h	j	k	l	m
n	p	r	s	t
v	w	x	y	z

Two Master Rules for Teaching Reading

Rule #1: Do not correct.
As soon as your student feels he is "wrong," the brain shuts down and learning stops. Instead of jumping in to correct your student, allow mistakes. Set up boundaries that are helpful. For example, don't glue until all pieces are laid in their spots with matching exercises. If your student reads a word or letter sound wrong, make a note to yourself to give a lesson on that sound before your next reading session at a neutral moment. Lastly, allow inventive spelling at this stage. Your student does not need to spell every word correctly to become a perfect speller later on. The practice of *writing* using sounds from memory is more important right now.

Rule #2: Do not ask your student to read back what he wrote.
This is a skill in itself, and when your student first starts writing (or building) words, he most likely won't be able to read them. If you ask for a skill he is not ready to master, it will discourage further work. Give your student the *practice of writing* without the burden of reading his inventive spelling and less than perfect handwriting, which are 100% appropriate at this stage.

Transitioning from Letter Sounds to Blending Words

Some students will easily blend the sounds /c/ /a/ /t/ into the word "cat," while others will say each sound individually and have a very hard time squishing them together into a single word.

For students who struggle with blending, here are a couple of things you can try.

1 - Use Your Finger
Invite your child to follow your finger as you place it under each letter sound. When you *hold your finger in place*, your child should *hold the sound*.
Here is an example:

Place your finger under c. Your child says /k/. Then quickly move your finger to under the letter a. Your child says, "aaaaaaaaaa," as you hold your finger under there for 3 seconds. Then move your finger to t and take it off the page. Your child will have said "caaaaaaat."

2 - Faster
Repeat the exercise, then ask your child to "say it fast!" If he is still saying, "k - a - t" as individual sounds, ask him to say it faster and faster until he can hear the word. Make sure you demonstrate for him if he is still struggling by sounding it out slowly and then more quickly.

Handwriting

There are handwriting exercises woven into this workbook to make it more Open-and-Go than traditional Montessori language shelf work.

We will practice handwriting in several ways:

1. **Lined Writing Spaces.**
   The green lined strips are a handwriting "control of error." Use the handwriting chart as needed on the back cover of the book as a reference or dry erase practice board.

2. **Drawings and Stencils.**
   In the "Draw and Write" sections, you will find a realistic story prompt to encourage your student to draw a picture using stencils (like the Montessori Shape Insets) or free-hand. Encourage your student to shade in his drawings very carefully using straight, non-overlapping lines using colored pencils. This will strengthen the student's hand for better pencil control and, in turn, better handwriting.

3. **Real-Life List Activities**
   In these list activities, your child writes an item on the blank, unlined space and then draws pictures of what he wrote. The pictures can be drawn after each item or at the end. These encourage writing for all students, but especially helps those who are not ready for the lines.

4. **Movable Alphabet Option**
   In each writing activity, you will find a reminder in the instructions that your student can use the movable alphabet to "write." If you want or need a permanent record of work, you can do the writing for your student by copying the exact sequence of letters your child "wrote" with the movable alphabet or invite your child to use alphabet stamps to copy the words. If you need a free download of a movable alphabet to print, head to montessoriforhomeschoolers.com where you will be able to download the **free "Montessori Homeschool Kickstarter Pack."**

Getting Started with the Montessori Pink Series Reading Workbook

Where do I start?
Getting started with this workbook is as easy as opening it up, reading the directions for the first lesson, and doing what is prompted with your student. Just go in order of the lessons, and you will be adding difficulty and new phonics sounds progressively. The lessons for Units 1-5 are repetitive, so you may find your child has little need of your directions for most lessons after completing Unit 1.

Can I make the lessons into shelf work?
Since this is a Montessori-inspired curriculum, I wanted to share with you the options you have for table-style *and* shelf-style learning. If you choose to use learning shelves, each lesson in this workbook is easily adaptable for a learning shelf. Here are some steps I would take if preparing the lessons for shelf work:

1. Cut, laminate, and arrange lesson on a tray.
2. Place activities from easiest to hardest. Easiest goes in the top left spot of the shelf, and hardest goes in the bottom right of the shelf, just like reading order. Using the materials in this workbook, you can simply place the work trays in lesson order. (Note: If you are working in a homeschool environment, you will have significantly fewer trays since you may have only one or two students working on this material.)
3. Make sure all needed "extras," like a movable alphabet, are accessible.

Should I keep the mini-books that we make throughout the curriculum?
This is completely up to you! If you do decide to keep them, an easy way to store the mini books is to glue an envelope to the inside back cover of the book. There are places inside the pages of the workbook itself to store the Readers, too!

How many lessons should my student complete each day?
This varies from child to child with maturity, age, and personality. If you would like, you can set a goal of one complete lesson, allowing your child to do more as his attention span improves or as he desires. The lessons are short - on purpose! Reading should be fun, and it should be practiced daily without bogging the child down with too much busywork.

Do you have suggestions for more beginning reader books?
Yes! The *Bob Books - Level 1 Readers* are perfect for this phonics progression. The Montessori Reading Games - Level 1, which is the prerequisite to this Workbook, were created to correspond with the new letters introduced in the *Bob Books* series.

A Special Note on Reading Aloud

Do it. Read aloud to your child for a minimum of 20 minutes per day. If she won't sit still (hint: most children do not sit perfectly still for story time), that is okay! Let her keep occupied with blocks, a puzzle, some play dough, or an art activity.

When I first started Montessori, I was hesitant to read anything to my child that was not based in reality. Children of a young age have not fully grasped concepts of truth and fiction, and they are still constructing their worlds. While this made sense, it still hurt my reading time. I fully believe that reading aloud is better than not reading aloud.

After more research, I have chosen to read as many "living books" to my children as possible, even if they have talking animals or fairytale creatures. I stay away from grim, dark books with scary elements. Living books are precious, helpful, and fun! So, find some "living books" and read to your children. If it has a talking dog, make sure you let your child know that the book is "make-believe" and the dog only talks because it is a story.

If you are determined to keep your read aloud time based in reality, do your best to choose books that still **tell a story.** Children like facts, but read aloud time is meant for *story*. Your children will learn so much more and be able to retain so much more if a book has all of the exciting components of story instead of merely listing facts and providing vibrant pictures.

Word-Picture Matching 1

Use the bottom half of the page for Lesson 1.1 and the top half of the page for Lesson 1.2.

Unit 1

cod	dam	sod
rim	bat	rat

Lesson 1.1 Picture to Word Matching

Cut apart the picture cards from page 7 and place the proper picture under each word. Paste when all pictures have been matched.

mat	cat	hat
dot	ham	cot

Lesson 1.2 Word to Picture Matching
Cut apart the word cards from page 7 and place the proper word under each picture. Paste when all words have been matched.

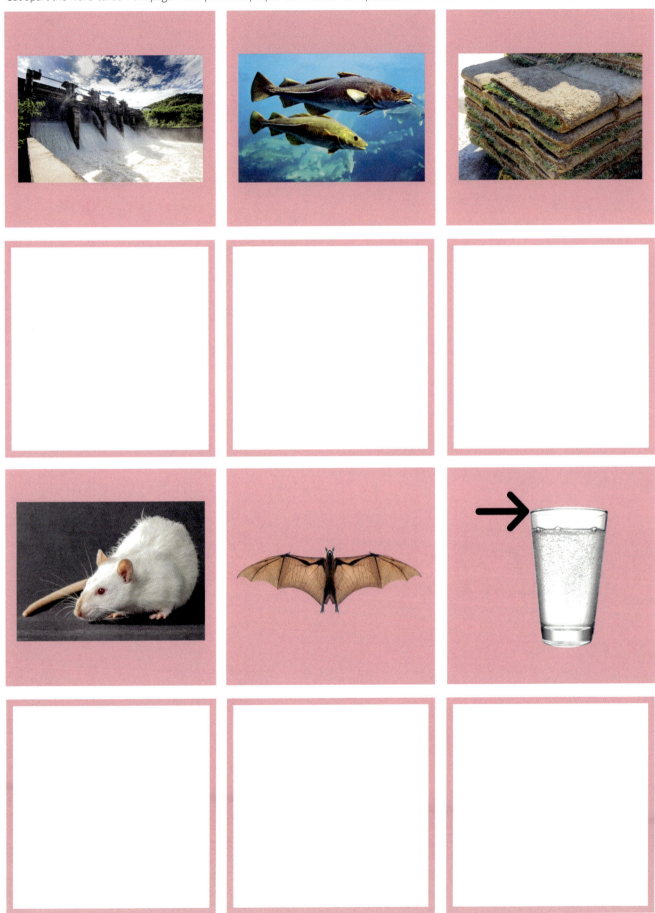

Lesson 1.3 Word Writing

Using a movable alphabet OR a pencil, invite your student to write the following words by sounding them out. Give your student access to the handwriting chart in the back of the book, as needed. Do not correct spelling or handwriting. If desired, your student can cut these out to make his or her own book. [Note: If your student needs a little extra guidance, it is extremely helpful to have your student first write the word using a movable alphabet then copy it onto the lined space.]

Lesson 1.4 Word Writing

Using a movable alphabet OR a pencil, invite your student to write the following words by sounding them out. Give your student access to the handwriting chart in the back of the book, as needed. Do not correct spelling or handwriting. If desired, your student can cut these out to make his or her own book.

Lesson 1.5 Secret Words

Cut along the dotted lines, and then fold the paper to cover each word. Invite your student to read each word as she uncovers it, one at a time, and then whisper the word to you.

Optional extension: Tell your student you are looking for a specific word on the list. Invite your student to uncover each word, one at a time. When she finds your word, tell her to whisper it to you then show you the word.

sat

had

Sam

sad

hat

cat

dot

Lesson 1.6 Action Game

Prep: Fold the flaps over these words (instead of the previous page).
Directions to student: Read and then act out each of the words. I will guess which word you are acting out.

sad

mad

hot

dot

sat

cat

hat

Lesson 1.7 Pink Booklet 1 — Cut, stack in order, and fold down the middle to make a booklet. Staple at spine. Invite your student to read it! Keep to re-read if there is interest later.

15

pink booklet
1

dot

cot

hot

ham

cod

Lesson 1.8 Draw and Write

Instructions: Draw a picture of a pig in the mud. Use free-form drawing, stencils, or the Montessori metal shape insets. Carefully color in your drawing with smooth, connected shading. Then **write** a sentence about what you drew!

You may need to help your student come up with a sentence. If your student needs to use the movable alphabet to write, that is perfectly fine! Don't correct spelling or punctuation. If you would like to record the story, you can take a picture of the written story and paste it onto the page under the drawing *or* write the story for your child by copying the story from the sentence he wrote with the movable alphabet.

Lesson 1.9 Make a List: Bake a Cake

[Note: This may need to be adapted for a non-home setting. Do what you can to make this a tangible experience!]

Instructions: To make writing and reading more meaningful, today take the time to invite your student to write out the ingredients needed to bake a cake. Invite your student to draw pictures of each ingredient next to the written words. (This will help your student "remember" what he wrote in case he isn't fluently able to read his own writing.)

Writing can be done using the movable alphabet with the teacher as a scribe *or* the student can write anywhere on this page. Encourage inventive spelling, and don't correct any wrong spelling. For example, "egz," "milc," and "flar" might be on the list (eggs, milk, flour.) After writing all of the ingredients your student already knows are inside a cake, you can use a recipe you have on hand or look one up to dictate missing ingredients. Then, take this list to the store to shop for ingredients with your student. Lastly, bake the cake together!

Word-Picture Matching 2

Unit 2

Use the bottom half of the page for Lesson 2.1 and the top half of the page for Lesson 2.2.

ram	gas	hog
tap	tag	pot

Lesson 2.1 Picture to Word Matching

Cut apart the picture cards from page 19 and place the proper picture under each word. Paste when all pictures have been matched.

mac	rod	dog
cob	rag	bag

Lesson 2.2 Word to Picture Matching

Cut apart the word cards from page 19 and place the proper word under each picture. Paste when all words have been matched.

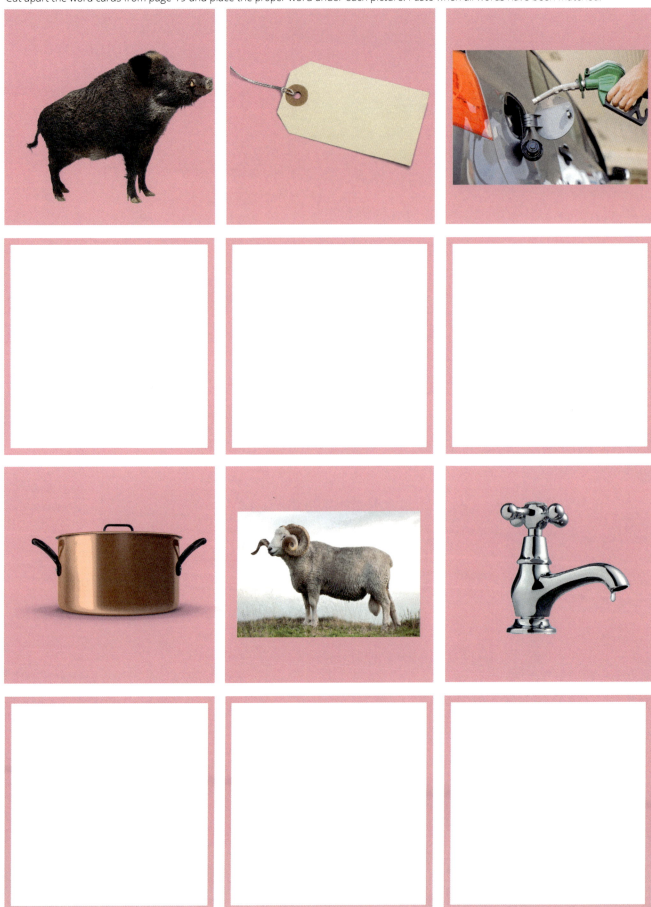

Lesson 2.3 Word Writing

Using a movable alphabet OR a pencil, invite your student to write the following words by sounding them out. Give your student access to the handwriting chart in the back of the book, as needed. Do not correct spelling or handwriting. If desired, your student can cut these out to make his or her own book.

Lesson 2.4 Word Writing

Using a movable alphabet OR a pencil, invite your student to write the following words by sounding them out. Give your student access to the handwriting chart in the back of the book, as needed. Do not correct spelling or handwriting. If desired, your student can cut these out to make his or her own book.

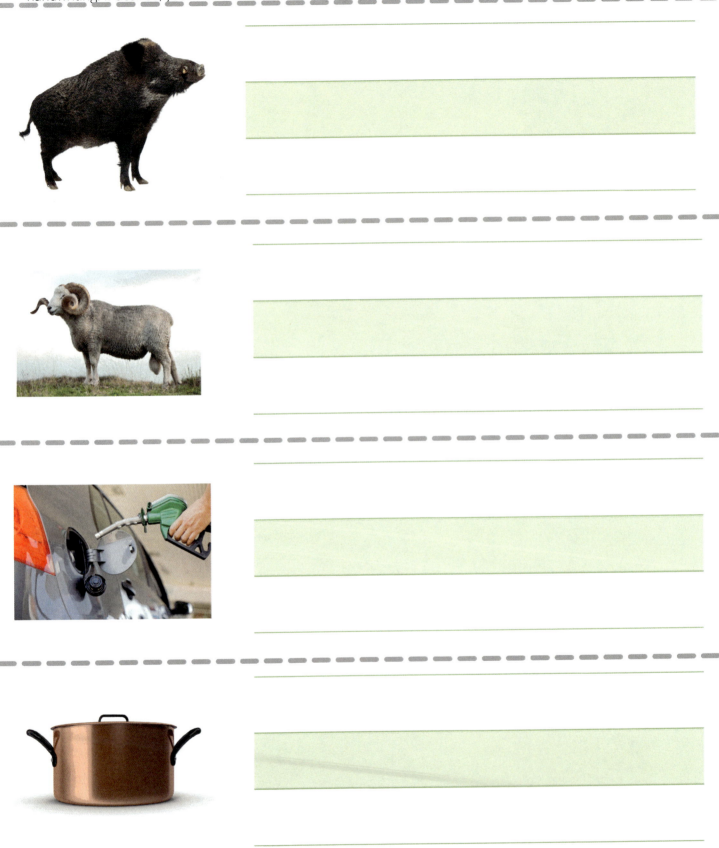

Lesson 2.5 Secret Words

Cut along the dotted lines, and then fold the paper to cover each word. Invite your student to read each word as she uncovers it, one at a time, and then whisper the word to you.

Optional extension: Tell your student you are looking for a specific word on the list. Invite your student to uncover each word, one at a time. When she finds your word, tell her to whisper it to you then show you the word.

rig

big

rib

bit

hit

hot

got

Lesson 2.6 Action Game

Prep: Fold the flaps over these words (instead of the previous page).
Directions to student: Read and then act out each of the words. I will guess which word you are acting out.

sit

tag

bat

dig

bit

hit

sob

Lesson 2.7
Pink Booklet 2

Cut, stack in order, and fold down the middle to make a booklet. Staple at spine. Invite your student to read it! Keep to re-read if there is interest later.

Lesson 2.8 Draw and Write

Instructions: Draw a picture of a big dog. Use free-form drawing, stencils, or the Montessori metal shape insets. Carefully color in your drawing with smooth, connected shading. Then **write** a sentence about what you drew!

You may need to help your student come up with a sentence. If your student needs to use the movable alphabet to write, that is perfectly fine! Don't correct spelling or punctuation. If you would like to record the story, you can take a picture of the written story and paste it onto the page under the drawing *or* write the story for your student by copying the story from the sentence he wrote with the movable alphabet.

Lesson 2.9 Make a List: Pack a Bag

[Note: This may need to be adapted for a non-home setting. Do what you can to make this a tangible experience!]

Instructions: To make writing and reading more meaningful, today take the time to invite your student to write out a list of items that he would need to pack to take a trip. This can be a long trip, like a vacation or trip to Grandma's, or a trip to the library or park. The key is to make it *real*. After making the list, help your student draw simple stick drawings next to the words he wrote. This helps with inventive spelling and allows students to "read" what they wrote when they aren't quite ready to read their own handwriting. Don't correct your student's spelling, but you can help segment words by breaking it down into its phonograms to assist him in finding the correct letters to use. (For example, "apple" is /a/ /p/ /l/. Your student might write "apl" or "apul" and that is fine!) After completing the list and the simple drawings, invite your student to take this list and use it to help guide his packing. Then, actually **go** to your destination! Writing and reading are *useful*, which is what your student has just proven by completing this exercise!

Word-Picture Matching 3

Use the bottom half of the page for Lesson 3.1 and the top half of the page for Lesson 3.2.

Unit 3

cup	*gum*	*pig*
gun	*pan*	*pin*

31

Lesson 3.1 Picture to Word Matching

Cut apart the picture cards from page 31 and place the proper picture under each word. Paste when all pictures have been matched.

wig	cop	mug

rug	bug	cap

Lesson 3.2 Word to Picture Matching

Cut apart the word cards from page 31 and place the proper word under each picture. Paste when all words have been matched.

34

Lesson 3.3 Word Writing

Using a movable alphabet OR a pencil, invite your student to write the following words by sounding them out. Give your student access to the handwriting chart in the back of the book, as needed. Do not correct spelling or handwriting. If desired, your student can cut these out to make his or her own book.

Lesson 3.4 Word Writing

Using a movable alphabet OR a pencil, invite your student to write the following words by sounding them out. Give your student access to the handwriting chart in the back of the book, as needed. Do not correct spelling or handwriting. If desired, your student can cut these out to make his or her own book.

Lesson 3.5 Secret Words

Cut along the dotted lines, and then fold the paper to cover each word. Invite your student to read each word as she uncovers it, one at a time, and then whisper the word to you.

Optional extension: Tell your student you are looking for a specific word on the list. Invite your student to uncover each word, one at a time. When she finds your word, tell her to whisper it to you then show you the word.

hug

nut

not

pun

rip

win

pod

Lesson 3.6 Action Game

Prep: Fold the flaps over these words (instead of the previous page).
Directions to student: Read and then act out each of the words. I will guess which word you are acting out.

pat

nod

tip

hug

sip

tap

nap

Lesson 3.7
Pink Booklet 3

Cut, stack in order, and fold down the middle to make a booklet. Staple at spine. Invite your student to read it! Keep to re-read if there is interest later.

39

Lesson 3.8 Draw and Write

Instructions: Draw a picture of a man chewing gum. Use free-form drawing, stencils, or the Montessori metal shape insets. Carefully color in your drawing with smooth, connected shading. Then **write** a sentence about what you drew!

You may need to help your student come up with a sentence. If your student needs to use the movable alphabet to write, that is perfectly fine! Don't correct spelling or punctuation. If you would like to record the story, you can take a picture of the written story and paste it onto the page under the drawing *or* write the story for your student by copying the story from the sentence he wrote with the movable alphabet.

Lesson 3.9 Make a List: All About Me

[Note: This may need to be adapted for a non-home setting. Do what you can to make this a tangible experience!]

Instructions: To make writing and reading more meaningful, today take the time to invite your student to write out a list of his or her characteristics. Start with the visible characteristics (eye color, hair color, height, age, etc.), and then move on to any other attributes, such as likes/dislikes, favorites (food, place to go, toy, outfit, etc.) Feel free to invite your student to use a movable alphabet, write with a pencil, or let you be the scribe. Inventive spelling is encouraged, and make sure to help your child segment words into their individual sounds if he struggles to write on his own. When the list is finished, invite your student to draw a self-portrait and add any other details to the picture!

Word-Picture Matching 4

Use the bottom half of the page for Lesson 4.1 and the top half of the page for Lesson 4.2.

sap	bun	top
pug	mop	jet

Lesson 4.1 Picture to Word Matching

Cut apart the picture cards from page 43 and place the proper picture under each word. Paste when all pictures have been matched.

jam	leg	fan
hen	fog	net

Lesson 4.2 Word to Picture Matching

Cut apart the word cards from page 43 and place the proper word under each picture. Paste when all words have been matched.

46

Lesson 4.3 Word Writing

Using a movable alphabet OR a pencil, invite your student to write the following words by sounding them out. Give your student access to the handwriting chart in the back of the book, as needed. Do not correct spelling or handwriting. If desired, your student can cut these out to make his or her own book.

47

Lesson 4.4 Word Writing

Using a movable alphabet OR a pencil, invite your student to write the following words by sounding them out. Give your student access to the handwriting chart in the back of the book, as needed. Do not correct spelling or handwriting. If desired, your student can cut these out to make his or her own book.

Lesson 4.5 Secret Words

Cut along the dotted lines, and then fold the paper to cover each word. Invite your student to read each word as she uncovers it, one at a time, and then whisper the word to you.

Optional extension: Tell your student you are looking for a specific word on the list. Invite your student to uncover each word, one at a time. When she finds your word, tell her to whisper it to you then show you the word.

jot

fat

lot

lit

pen

fed

let

Lesson 4.6 Action Game

Prep: Fold the flaps over these words (instead of the previous page).
Directions to student: Read and then act out each of the words. I will guess which word you are acting out.

jog

beg

lug

fed

met

pen

fin

Lesson 4.7
Pink Booklet 4

Cut, stack in order, and fold down the middle to make a booklet. Staple at spine. Invite your child to read it! Keep to re-read if there is interest later.

51

pink booklet
4

tap and sap
21 2

bug on log
19 4

hot sun
17 6

hot mug
15 8

rat and cat
13 10

Lesson 4.8 Draw and Write

Instructions: Draw a picture of a red bag. Use free-form drawing, stencils, or the Montessori metal shape insets. Carefully color in your drawing with smooth, connected shading. Then **write** a sentence about what you drew! Use your imagination to think what could be inside the red bag!

You may need to help your student come up with a sentence. If your student needs to use the movable alphabet to write, that is perfectly fine! Don't correct spelling or punctuation. If you would like to record the story, you can take a picture of the written story and paste it onto the page under the drawing *or* write the story for your child by copying the story from the sentence he wrote with the movable alphabet.

Lesson 4.9 Make a List: My Day

[Note: This may need to be adapted for a non-home setting. Do what you can to make this a tangible experience!]

Instructions: To make writing and reading more meaningful, today take the time to invite your student to write out the activities he/she does throughout the day! Start with waking up, and see how many activities your student can think to add to the list. Feel free to invite your student to use a movable alphabet, write with a pencil, or let you be the scribe. Inventive spelling is encouraged, and make sure to help your student segment words into their individual sounds if he struggles to write on his own. When the list is finished, invite your student to draw pictures of each of the parts of his day.

Word-Picture Matching 5

Unit 5

Use the bottom half of the page for Lesson 5.1 and the top half of the page for Lesson 5.2.

ten	lid	kit
kid	van	fox

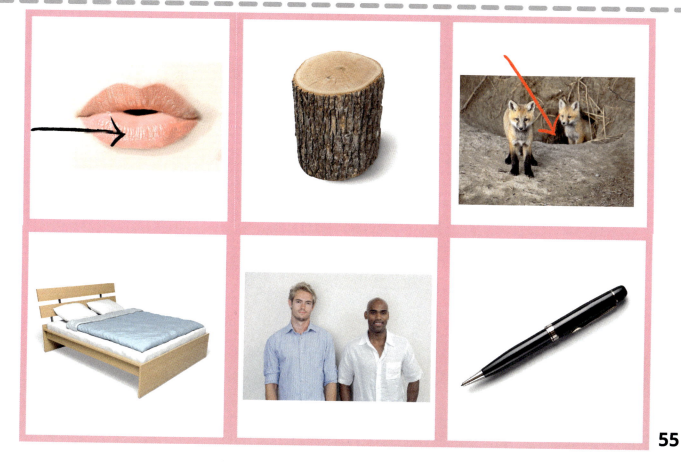

Lesson 5.1 Picture to Word Matching

Cut apart the picture cards from page 55 and place the proper picture under each word. Paste when all pictures have been matched.

men	bed	log
pen	lip	den

Lesson 5.2 Word to Picture Matching

Cut apart the word cards from page 55 and place the proper word under each picture. Paste when all words have been matched.

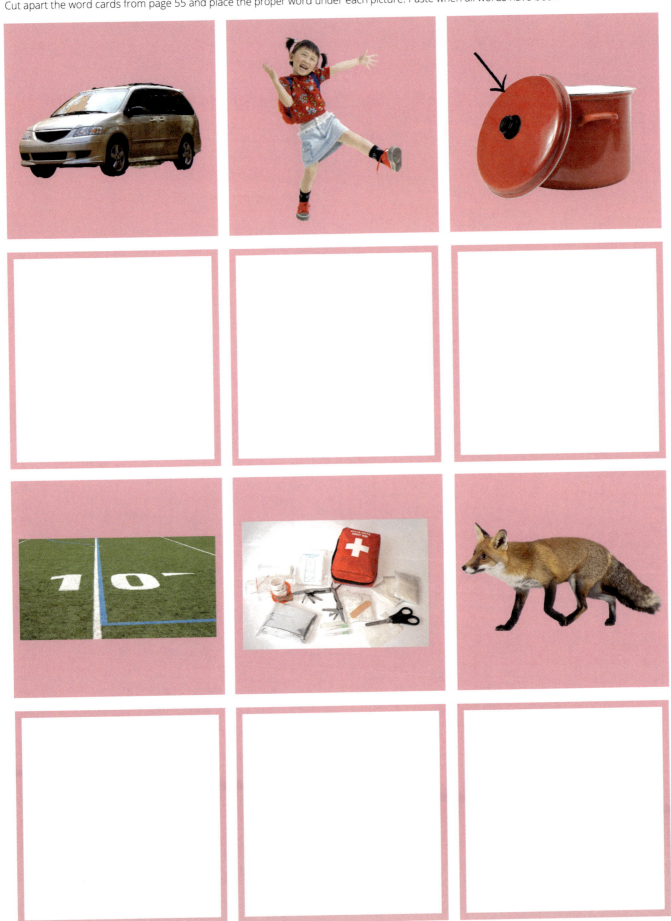

Lesson 5.3 Word Writing

Using a movable alphabet OR a pencil, invite your student to write the following words by sounding them out. Give your student access to the handwriting chart in the back of the book, as needed. Do not correct spelling or handwriting. If desired, your student can cut these out to make his or her own book.

Lesson 5.4 Word Writing

Using a movable alphabet OR a pencil, invite your student to write the following words by sounding them out. Give your student access to the handwriting chart in the back of the book, as needed. Do not correct spelling or handwriting. If desired, your student can cut these out to make his or her own book.

Lesson 5.5 Secret Words

Cut along the dotted lines, and then fold the paper to cover each word. Invite your student to read each word as she uncovers it, one at a time, and then whisper the word to you.

Optional extension: Tell your student you are looking for a specific word on the list. Invite your student to uncover each word, one at a time. When she finds your word, tell her to whisper it to you then show you the word.

vat

fix

yap

rap

lug

pox

fit

Lesson 5.6 Action Game

Prep: Fold the flaps over these words (instead of the previous page).
Directions to student: Read and then act out each of the words. I will guess which word you are acting out.

yap

vex

dip

zap

zip

kiss

lit

Pink Booklet 5

Cut, stack in order, and fold down the middle to make a booklet. Staple at spine. Invite your student to read it! Keep to re-read if there is interest later.

hat and sax
1 / 22

box on top
3 / 20

fox in den
5 / 18

jet in sun
7 / 16

big yak
9 / 14

zip up
11 / 12

pink booklet
5

fun lad

man runs

bug on kid

red van

rat and cat

Lesson 5.8 Draw and Write

Instructions: Draw a picture of your favorite animal in its home. Use free-form drawing, stencils, or the Montessori metal shape insets. Carefully color in your drawing with smooth, connected shading. Then **write** a sentence about what you drew!

You may need to help your student come up with a sentence. If your student needs to use the movable alphabet to write, that is perfectly fine! Don't correct spelling or punctuation. If you would like to record the story, you can take a picture of the written story and paste it onto the page under the drawing *or* write the story for your student by copying the story from the sentence he wrote with the movable alphabet.

Lesson 5.9 Make a List: In the Mail

[Note: This may need to be adapted for a non-home setting. Do what you can to make this a tangible experience!]

Instructions: To make writing and reading more meaningful, today take the time to invite your student to write out a list of things his or her family receives in the mail!

Feel free to invite your student to use a movable alphabet, write with a pencil, or let you be the scribe. Inventive spelling is encouraged, and make sure to help your student segment words into their individual sounds if he struggles to write on his own. When the list is finished, invite your student to draw pictures of each of the items.

Lesson 6.1
Reading Lists 1 & 2

Invite your student to read one full list at a time, folding the page in half to isolate each list. Keep track of the lists your student has read by marking the corresponding boxes.

Unit 3

☐ List 1
☐ List 2

cat

hat

bat

fat

sat

mat

pat

rat

jet

bet

get

let

met

pet

set

vet

Lesson 6.2
Reading Lists 3 & 4

☐ List 3
☐ List 4

kit

bit

fit

hit

lit

pit

sit

wit

pot

bot

cot

dot

got

hot

jot

lot

Lesson 6.3
Reading Lists 5 & 6

☐ List 5
☐ List 6

hut

but

cut

gut

jut

nut

rut

tut

jam

bam

cam

dam

ham

ram

sam

yam

Lesson 6.4
Reading Lists 7 & 8

☐ List 7
☐ List 8

pen

ben

den

hen

men

ten

yen

zen

lid

bid

did

fid

hid

kid

mid

rid

Lesson 6.5
Reading List 7

List 9

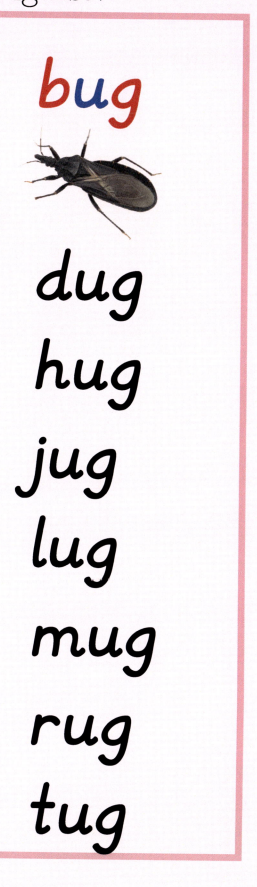

bug

dug

hug

jug

lug

mug

rug

tug

71

Lesson 6.6 Picture to Phrase Match

Invite your student to cut out the picture squares from the bottom of the page, then place into the corresponding spots by first reading the phrase and then finding the corresponding picture. Glue all pictures when finished.

	bat and ball
	red wig on dog
	zip up
	nap on bed

Lesson 6.7 Phrase to Picture Match

Invite your student to cut out the phrase strips from the bottom of the page, then place into the corresponding spots by first reading the phrase and then finding the corresponding picture. Glue when finished.

box is on top

pig is in mud

kid has fan

cat and rat

Lesson 6.8 I Can Read: Book 1, "Tom"

Prepare Material: Cut out the book along the pink lines. Stack the double-sided pages in order, with the pink cover facing down on the bottom of the stack and stacking the pages in order. You should see pages 1, 3, 5, 7, and 9 on the bottom left corners, with 1 on the bottom and 9 on top. Then fold. Staple at the spine.

Prepare student: Before reading, show the child the article "a." Show the child when it is by itself, you say the name of the letter A. Point to it and say, "When this sound is by itself, we say, a."

Next show the child the new sound "th" and "Th." Point. and say, "This says /th/." Then show your student the word "the." Invite your student to sound it out and blend the word. Help if needed.

Lastly, point out the capital letter "T." Tell your student it says /t/ unless it is in the word "The," like you just practiced.

a

th
Th

the
The

Tom

The kid is Tom.

1   18

Tom is six.

3   16

75

Fold up flap from reverse page to store "Tom" book here.

Tom is not sad.

Mom will fix it!

Tom is sad.

Lesson 6.9 Picture to Phrase Match

Invite your student to cut out the picture squares from the bottom of the page, then place into the corresponding spots by first reading the phrase and then finding the corresponding picture. Glue only after all pictures have been placed.

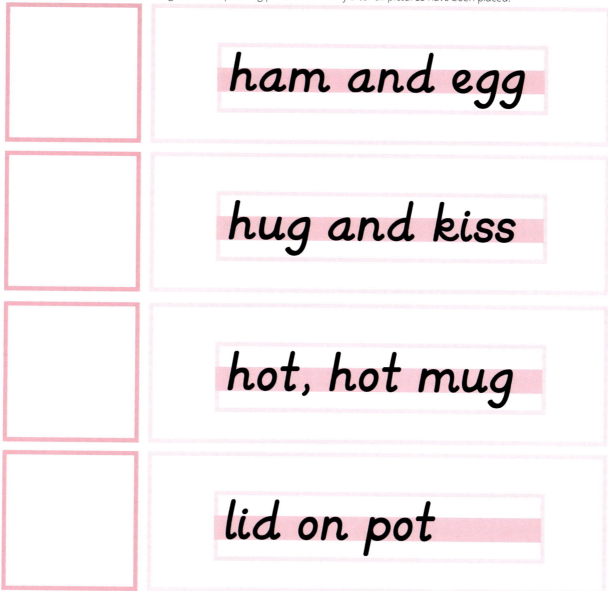

ham and egg

hug and kiss

hot, hot mug

lid on pot

Lesson 6.10 Phrase to Picture Match

Invite your student to cut out the phrase strips from the bottom of the page, then place them onto the corresponding spots by first reading the phrase and then finding the corresponding picture. Glue phrases only after all have been matched.

Lesson 6.11 I Can Read: Book 2, "Peg"

Prepare Material: Cut out the book along the pink lines. Stack the double-sided pages in order, with the pink cover facing down on the bottom of the stack and stacking the pages in order. You should see pages 1, 3, 5, 7, and 9 on the bottom left corners, with 1 on the bottom and 9 on top. Then fold. Staple at the spine.

Prepare student: Before reading, review the new sound "th" and "Th." Point. and say, "This says /th/." hen show your student the word "the." Invite your student to sound it out. Help if needed.
Practice reading "the" and "The" together.
Next, show your student the capital letter "B." Say, "This says, /b/."

th   the   b
Th   The   B

Peg

fold up to store book

Peg had a hat.

①   ⑱

The hat was red.

③   ⑯

Fold up flap from reverse page to store "Peg" book here.

The red hat fell.

The hat got wet.

Mud got on it.

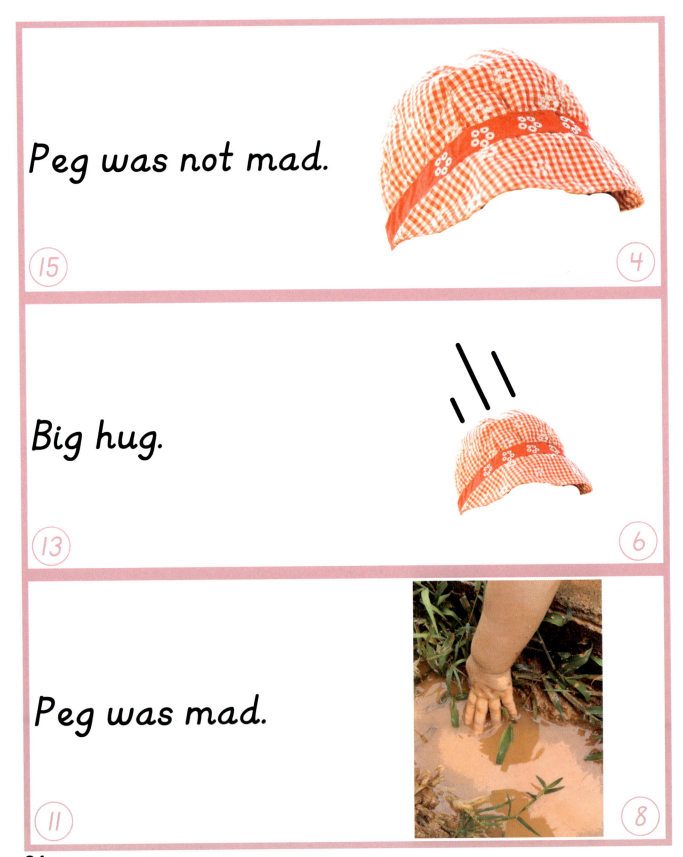

Lesson 6.12 Picture to Phrase Match

Invite your student to cut out the picture squares from the bottom of the page, then place onto the corresponding spots by first reading the phrase and then finding the corresponding picture. Glue down after all pictures have been matched.

hop on top

mop up mud

tip a hat

fun, wet dog

Lesson 6.13 Phrase to Picture Match

Invite your student to cut out the phrase strips from the bottom of the page, then place into the corresponding spots by first reading the phrase and then finding the corresponding picture. Glue down phrases after all have been matched.

Lesson 6.14 I Can Read: Book 3, "Jan"

Prepare Material: Cut out the book along the pink lines. Stack the double-sided pages in order, with the pink cover facing down on the bottom of the stack and stacking the pages in order. You should see pages 1, 3, 5, 7, and 9 on the bottom left corners, with 1 on the bottom and 9 on top. Then fold. Staple at the spine.

Prepare student: Before reading, review the sound "th" and "Th." Point. and say, "This says /th/." Then show your student the word "the." Invite your student to sound "the" and "The." Help if needed.

Next, show your child the capital letters "R" and "D." Point to each and say, "This says /r/." "This says /d/."

| th | the | r | d |
| Th | The | R | D |

Jan (upside down, on pink cover)

fold up to store book

Jan has a dog.

① ⑱

The dog is big.

③ ⑯

Fold up flap from reverse page to store "Jan" book here.

Jan

The end.

The dog runs.

Jan runs.

The big dog is fun.

The cat runs.

Run, run, run.

Dad is fun.

Name:_____
Date Completed:_____

Pink Series Completed

I can read books!

I did it! I worked hard and completed my
<u>Montessori Pink Series Reading Workbook!</u>

I am most proud of myself for

I love how

I have proven I am capable of

Handwriting Chart

Remove and laminate for reference and dry-erase tracing practice.

a b c d e f g h i

j k l m n o p q r

s t u v w x y z

Other Publications by Katie Key

Montessori Reading Games - Level 1
Teach your child the 26 sounds of the letters of the alphabet using a system of games. Cursive and Print font options. Digital download.

https://montessoriforhomeschoolers.com/products/montessori-reading-games-1

Montessori Christian Homeschool Preschool Curriculum
A step-by-step guide to preparing, purchasing, and presenting a full Montessori curriculum that is Christ-centered to your child. Includes: Bible, Reading and Writing, Math, Sensorial, Shapes and Colors, and more! Digital download.

https://montessoriforhomeschoolers.com/products/montessori-christian-homeschool-preschool-curriculum

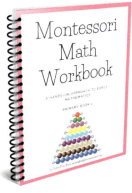

Montessori Math Workbook - Primary Book 1
A hands-on open-and-go Montessori math curriculum. This workbook uniquely takes the Montessori concrete materials and puts them on paper, so your child can sit with a pencil, scissors, and glue, and concretely manipulate, touch, and visualize numbers, creating a strong math foundation using just this workbook. We cover conceptualizing numbers 0-100 in a Montessori sequence through many hands-on and visual activities.Choose the digital download or printed workbook.

https://montessoriforhomeschoolers.com/products/montessori-math-workbook

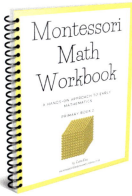

Montessori Math Workbook - Primary Book 2
In this Open-and-Go curriculum, your child will be introduced to the following math concepts through concrete manipulation of materials: Squaring Numbers 1-10 using the Montessori Short Bead Chains, Counting 1-1000 linearly and Cubing 10, Decimal System and Place Value using the Montessori Golden Beads, Recognizing and Forming One to Four Digit Numbers, Addition, Subtraction, Multiplication, and Division of Four Digit Numbers using the Golden Beads, and A Unique Looping Review System to review previously covered concepts from Primary Books 1 and 2 to work toward full mastery!

https://montessoriforhomeschoolers.com/products/montessori-math-workbook-primary-book-2

Made in the USA
Middletown, DE
31 August 2023

37731812R00055